The Beachcomber's Report

By the same author:

Kelpdings

The Beachcomber's Report

Paul Maddern

Templar Poetry

Published in 2010 by Templar Poetry

Templar Poetry in an imprint of Delamide & Bell

Fenelon House

Kingsbridge Terrace

58 Dale Road, Matlock, Derbyshire

DE4 3NB

www.templarpoetry.co.uk

ISBN 978-1-906285-33-3

A CIP catalogue record of this book is available from the British Library

Typeset by Pliny
Graphics by Paloma Violet

Printed in India

For Hettie & Jon, Jane & Ken

Acknowledgements

Acknowledgements are due the editors of the following publications in which a number of these poems, or versions of them, have appeared: *The Bermuda Anthology of Poetry* (Vol. 2), *Black Mountain Review*, *The Caribbean Writer*, *Fortnight*, *From a Small Back Room: A Festschrift for Ciaran Carson* (Netherlea Press, 2008), *Incertus* (Netherlea Press, 2007), *Iota*, *Landing Places* (Dedalus Press, 2010), *Poetry Ireland Review*, *Post*, *The Shop, Ulster Tatler,* and *The Yellow Nib* (Vol. 4). Several were included in a pamphlet, *Kelpdings*, also with Templar Poetry, 2009.

Thanks are due to the Arts Council of Northern Ireland for a Support for Individual Artists Award, 2009. With special thanks to Ciaran Carson, Sinéad Morrissey, Ian Sansom and Jane Weir.

Contents

look there
to the north-east,
the ocean rolling
    constant:

the nimble seals'
bright sport,
the sea-swelling
    fullness

      —after 10th-Century Irish, Anon

32° 19' 59" N / 64° 45' 0" W

Pull back the mantle of the ocean
and strange the ocean.
Bring down the ether from the sky
and fable the sky.
Assemble dot by dot the stars
and cipher the stars
and strange the ocean
and fable the sky.
Pull back the mantle of the ocean,
bring down the ether from the sky.

Islanded

Why return to this avenue
that opens to daylight on the beach,
where I can pick mangoes and sink
my feet—the one, the other—into the blue
of familiar then unfamiliar tidal pools?

Always from the horizon come
polluted ranks of sails and liners and planes.
If defined by the loss of degrees in these sub-topics,
still an invading force to rival great armadas,
still vicious in their capacity.

To guard the shore I have sculpted a wall of heroes
from wet sand, but have also watched them
spent by tides. I have tried kisses and more
as charms to save them all,
my indigenous Canutes and Calibans.

Undaunted, I dispatch another man-o-war,
its varicose tendrils to slip back undetected
on the undercurrent and charge the ocean
with the force of my convictions:
defend, if it can, this isolation.

I tear a ripe mango from its tree
and splash in blue pools. I have my answer
and there was no invasion. The day
tucks into history. Canvas after canvas
sails close by, before the pockmarked moon.

Kelpdings

At low tide I put the slip into boat-slip
and landed my ass on the line
where green algae gives way to brown.
Reduced to sea level view I found
exotic kelp frond calligraphies scrawled
over every degree of Harbour Blue:
insular majuscules, Gothic minuscules,
Carolingians, copperplates, bastard hands;
the curlicues and cuneiforms of fancy
shaping bywords for baptism and resurrection.

Marginalia

the small bandit's
sharp directive
from the swell of
    its yellow breast:

kiskadee flares
on plantations—
liberty bursts
    from lemon trees

On Being Told by an Irishman that I Overuse 'Oleander'

If I agree, will you then permit me the use of avocado, mango, palmetto, Sargasso, wahoo, pompano, longtail, loquat, mangrove, grotto, coral, and cahow (the word we gave the only indigenous creature to be found on our small island), bougainvillea, pawpaw, cassava, barracuda, bermudiana (a tiny wild iris that is almost an adjective), frangipani, amaryllis, hibiscus, kiskadee, skink, cereus, but most of all cedar? Can I keep cedar? Because we have a strain of cedar that like the cahow is indigenous to our island and to which we have given the island's name. And this cedar, the most fragrant, the most buoyant of cedars, rich grained and producing oils, is in danger. It was once the bronzed bones of whalers and dinghies, and prize-seeking sloops that outstripped what the world had to offer. And while it played its part in the fabric of flogging posts, gibbets, stocks, stakes and pyres, when the blight of '46 destroyed almost all the trees, our island mourned. We still mourn and preserve what remains. Today, for example, it is a sin to burn cedar as firewood. Instead we admire its antique nature, found in the ceiling beams and box pews of St. Peter's (the oldest Anglican church in the Western Hemisphere), in ceremonial chairs and boardroom tables, the banisters of grand staircases, dressers, sideboards, linen chests, captains' chests, window- picture- and bed-frames and a few surviving household items: candle holders, fruit bowls, butter-paddles, drinking cups, lace bobbins, even doll's heads, knitting needles, crotchet hooks and toothpicks. And if you say it is cheapened by the knick-knack paperweights, letter openers, bookmarkers, shark-oil barometers, coasters, puzzle-cups, pens, pendants and broaches that the island trades with tourists, I will answer that our craftsmen still value the grain and save from scrap the art of tradition. So, can I keep cedar? You see:

> wise men are surplus
> we've allspice, oleander
> our cribs are cedar

Pervasions

> the women testing
> *Easter Lily* and *Jasmine*
> will be tourists

beyond lead glass
untended hibiscus grows
wild then seminal

> confection-petalled
> frangipani sweetens
> alfresco diners

in china pomanders
lavender antiques
the matriarch's boudoir

> religion distilled –
> passionflower's complicity
> loads votive candles

cereus unwraps
elusive taunts of bloom
for night watchmen

> (note: hot moped seats
> nip in the bud tender haikus
> on pale half-moons)

Bodysurf

—for Erin

To understand everything about the swell—
how on a given day the seventh in the cycle
provides the greatest chance to ride to shore
if caught where the rip collides with the surge,
where the wave pries a mouth wide
and prepares to heave its travelled miles—
to understand the moment of submission,
when to dive in and up the crest
in order to avoid a rabid tumble,
to be flung skyward out the other side
falling yards into the trough and humbled—
to understand that we're aligned
to leave behind horizons to the climbing wall,
hunched and turned three quarters,
believing that the travelling momentum
is such we'll be absorbed and pulled along,
so someone watching oceans from a towel
might raise herself a little on one elbow
and to her partner whisper, *Dolphins.*

Postamble

On Sunday walks beneath pink oleander
I'd let loose a week of stored up chat.
You'd select a stick from fallen branches
littering our path to Grape Bay Beach,
strip the remnant twigs and snap it
to the perfect height for your colonial stride,
for the rhythmic flicking out before
then regimental poke into adopted soil.

> The war-filled man on Newlyn's pier
> had chucked the mackerel for exotic species.

From our tropic shore we watched the barracuda
cross the panoramic window of the breaking wave,
gazed on coral reefs where parrot fish would ape
the sergeant majors' nibbling drill,
and Prospero's son glimpsed his father weave
the dreams he heard in shells, holding them holy.
Then, adopting to the island's pace,
hand in hand we combed the tidal margins.

> Without you now on Newlyn's pebble beach,
> I want support and search for sticks.

I know your row but not the house's number.
Some cousin's on the hill behind.
Godmother's gone. Her shop, renamed, remains.
Jack the crab and crayfish man, best friend
who should have been best man is also dead.
His factory stands beside the stream where as a boy
you fished for trout, fell, and scarred your knee.
The village tour has brought these pieces back to me.

I see the ailing Gulf Stream
still provides for palm trees on the green.

So, if trawlers' gulls won't call for longtails
over deep Atlantic seas, I'll still mate them.
If Cornwall's trees are unfamiliar, I'll rename them:
what might be elms become Bermuda cedars
and may-be-oaks feign pleasure to be casuarinas.
But we share an artist's light: though these bathers
don't lie down on coral sands, they still burn.
And a man who rambles finds a stick to aid him.

Would you accept the branch I hold?
I hesitate, but poke it in adopted soil.

The Last Act

A steam scrim climbs
    calabash high
off baked asphalt
    raising a trompe l'œil
of colonial house with garden,
    surround verandas
in laissez faire repair,
    shutters unhinged.

Neglected magnolias,
    those old retainers,
are left to petal dust
    and trace their roots
back to the gloom
    of the garden's vanishing point
where crabgrass meets
    sand, ocean and thundering sky.

In the foreground
    an old man mimes shoo away
to a child stepping
    clean from noon rains,
an audience standing its ground,
    anticipatory,
waiting for asphalt to dry
    and the scene to crumple.

Walsingham Cave

Midwinter light enters the slashed mouth
of the calcified grotto playing over draperies
and sapphire waters still as the pilgrim
who touches the limestone bones of the saint
and hears the confessional echo of the sepulchre,
the mineral-drip from stalactites
into the font where deposed idols lie,
joined in their drowning
by day-trekkers seeking absolution
who fall short in their devotions,
for casual trespass in the blind eyes of true cave-dwellers—
cyclopoids and calanoids, ostracods and decapods,
the *Bermudamysis speluncola* of the phylum Arthropoda—
cannot be forgiven lightly and demands recompense,
the cost evident in bloated torsos, trapped limbs,
armies of dashed skulls and women's tresses
all veiled in the quiet but betrayed to a believer
who waits until light departs the mouth,
who approaches empty-handed without guides or torches,
abandoning the tourists' paraphernalia,
the pilgrim who crouches on a poolside rock
shoeless and absorbed.

Jane,

It's Maundy Thursday,
the day of groundwork
for the Passion.

Shallow clay bowls are filled
with scented waters to wash
the feet of servants and masters.

Resurrections and Processionals
are made to gleam, prayer cushions
brushed for penitents.

Oils are warmed for anointing,
the Blessed Sacrament carried
to its place of reposition.

Every altar is stripped bare
except the Altar of Repose,
draped only in unblemished linens.

Antidoron trays are polished,
fresh-baked loaves torn
and readied for consecration.

Five-hundred Easter lilies, pre-arranged
and left outside, will tomorrow drown
the High Altar in perfect blooms.

And you, performing these duties,
pause only at midnight to mark
the start of our collective vigil.

Recension: *i.m.*

And a certain woman, named Lydia, a seller of purple, of the city
of Thyatira, one who worshiped God, heard us: whose heart the
Lord opened (Acts 16)

I

Creeping morning glory
  makes a memory of forms:
a safety curtain
  covers the veranda,
your cedar bench
  is now upholstered,
the Roman general
  sports a purple crown.
The depression
  of an ornamental pond
just survives,
  vines spilling from
the water pourer's urn.
  Indefinite lips
untouched by flowers
  overlay the leaves
with limestone dust.

> *All the way to Tucker's Town,*
> *Drinking rum and falling down.*
>
> *All the way round Harrington Sound,*
> *One wheel carriage rolling round.*

Your sons and the ground
  are ripe for conversion:
Robert's shock-still

beneath bougainvillea
that crowds the wall
   and halves the light;
Jamie studies passionflowers
   for resurrection's mysteries.
But the lavenders are fading
   and amethyst petals fall
to the morning glory floor
   that takes the memory of forms.

> *All the way to Mangrove Bay,*
> *There the old maids go to stay.*

> *All the way 'round Bailey's Bay,*
> *Fish and Taters all the day.*

Lead me not away.
   Take me by the hand
to reacquaint with passion
   all that's buried near.
I will not follow fashion
   in this hostile land
that cannot see the form
   beneath the winding sheet.
Teach me not to fear,
   to remember each eroding year
that serves to take me
   far from here.
Teach me how to bless
   what they have given—
the purpose for revision.

All the way to Crow Lane side,
Nothing there but foolish pride.

All the way to Spanish Point,
There the times are out of joint.

The sky is a tumbling wall
Before which doubters fall.

Gone are the childish cares
And gone are the innocent airs.

II

We're no more children climbing trees
than there are voices singing.

Jamie topples the general,
blinds an eye,
smashes his skull.

He tears down the curtain,
strips vines from the urn
and they fall away.

Only a little way left to go
before childish cares and innocent airs
are stripped, stripped away.

Robert unearths relics:
the faithful spaniel's skull, one flip-flop,
pill dispensers, golfing gloves.

Leaves are summer's yellowed tissue kites.
They are fall light.
They are everywhere.

We're no more children climbing trees
than there are voices singing.

The sky is a tumbling wall
before which doubters fall
and angels rise

like summer's yellowed tissue kites,
the memories of form.

III

Lydia, your purples are arrayed,
   silks rolled out, banners unfurled,

our hair is shaken loose,
   every stone is rolled away.

Our old songs are given an airing.
  They have fared well,

performed for memory's sake,
  then no more:

> *This is my finger*
> *This is my thumb*
> *This is my body*
> *This is my blood*
> *My blood and my body*

My body and blood
Gobble them up
Swallow them down
Smile and be merry
Then pass them around.

And now water pours
  from the water pourer's urn.

   There is joy
     in the kiskadee's call.

       And morning glories trumpet.
         Listen, they are blaring.

Codcakes and Kites

—for Jane Weir

After Maundy Thursday supper
rinse the block of salted cod.
Lower into a glass bowl
filled with tepid water.
Glance occasionally to check
the process of desalination.
When the water has clouded
drain then refill and re-soak.
Ensure you rise
once in the night
to repeat this process.

On Good Friday morning
drain into a colander.
Flake the cod.
Boil six of the freshest eggs,
the same of potatoes.
Now peel your three bananas
and, slicing lengthways,
spread over paper towel
allowing them to bleed moisture
in the way of zucchini and aubergine.
Season with pepper to temper the sugars.

Gather the children,
yours and the neighbours',
choosing one who can be trusted
to hold the Bermuda kite –
completed days before so the glue,
securing lozenges of multicoloured tissues
to the eight-spoke balsa frame

and its intricate string web,
will have hardened to the point
where the kite can have
a good chance against air.

Choose a patch of grass on which
the dew has evaporated.
Too many times I have witnessed
tissue kites crash onto damp ground.
Then, if the skies are clear,
with only moderate winds,
send the kite bearer down the garden
holding the kite at waist-level ready
to be thrown skyward in one unrushed gesture.
And make certain the knotted torn-sheet tail
is coiled at the feet for its untangled rise.

Check the tension is loose.
Too taut a string will allow
the kite no freedom to choose
breeze and direction.

Then, only on your signal,
when your wetted finger dries,
when all around you is still,
should the release of the kite
and the measured tug on the string
and the running backward
and the ascension
and the cheering
and the cheering
and the cheering begin.

When the kite is safely airborne,
the string paid out
and the rota for control arranged,
slip away.

The potatoes and eggs will have cooled.
Chop them roughly, adding
dill, tarragon and flat-leaf parsley.
Handfuls and handfuls and handfuls.
Sea salt to taste. Pepper. More pepper?
Several good pinches of paprika.
Then, using a table fork, mash together
with the cod and, yes, the bananas.
Take a palmful of the mixture
and shape into thick patties.
Dust each with plain flour.

Place in a frying pan
in which clarified butter sizzles.
Brown to gold on both sides.
Set aside and repeat until
the last is done, the aromas
just released and just wild.
While they bake in a hot oven
(I suggest twenty minutes)
go somewhere quiet to change
into starched cottons.
Add a simple tie or ribbon.

Then open a window
to a sweep of sky and children
and before you call them in
to prepare your table,
to partake,

pause and look up
to observe the light-rich
jewelled heads
of hundreds of snakes
swaying, swaying, swaying.
And be mesmerized.

Sunrise

—*after Wallace Stevens*

Empty ocean is best. Empty sky is best. Empty
except for my singular shore, squatting low
so the island's horizon curves on the eye,
so the wrapping of surf around my feet
is the touch to draw me out,
is the touch to draw me out by tides
and I swim, swim and wallow in the dawn.

Beachcomber's Report

The best place to hear the ocean in a shell
is at a plain wooden desk in a bare room,
your eyes closed, knowing that if open
they would overlook the sound
you're trying to remember.

If you're on a beach checking driftwood
for texture, density and weight, stop.
Take the pieces to the fireside and just before burning
smell them, then rub your index finger along the grain.
That's when you will value their assets best.

When you pick up an imperfect green glass
lobsterpot float, carry it to a distant beach
where such things do not exist and drop it
implausibly beyond the high-tide mark
for locals to puzzle over.

Barbie heads, Ken torsos, Cabbage Patch fingers
are best buried in identikit suburban yards,
forgotten, save for a vague feeling
a writer might one day dig a bed for roses
and imagine non-existent children.

Should you retrieve the message from the bottle,
hide the note in a library frequented by academics,
within a dry encyclopaedia –
Biographie Générale 35-36: Mer-Mur ?
Check from time to time if it has disappeared.

Collect frayed orange nylon rope
and pay someone who knits the going rate
for a sackcloth-and-ashes jumper,
ideal for sitting in that bare room
listening for the ocean in a shell.

And when all of this has been accomplished
burn the desk, scatter the driftwood cinders,
throw all floats and doll parts back to the sea,
unravel the jumper, and travel to Bermuda
primed to search for Prospero's Book.

Ferro et Flammis

There is no written law.
Powhatan's will is law.
Obeyed not only as a king
But esteemed as a half-god,
At his pleasure he despoils his people.

For his own house he takes four fifths
Of the wheat, fish, fowl, skins and roots.
He is proud and insolent, a great tyrant.
For a man from the Inns of Court,
Such as I, this last facet must be despised.

And yet these candles are like those made
Of the finest Shropshire pines
Found between Oswestry and Ellesmere,
This wine from grapes as luscious
As those in villages between Amiens and Paris.

Yes, the *politique carriage* lingers.
Even near his eightieth year
Powhatan is a goodly man, not shrinking.
But it is the majesty
Of an old, uncivil prince.

If he sprang from the womb indifferent white,
His skin is now coloured mulberry, like sodden quince.
Thin grey hair hangs to his shoulder, there remains
The trace of a beard and his face has a sad aspect,
Echoed in the song he sings for me:

Mattanerew shashashewaw erawango pechecoma
Whe Tassantassa inoshashaw yehockan pocosack
Whe whe yah ha ha ne he wittowa wittowa

*

He has no open quarrel with us,
But I believe this born of a fear
We intend to take away his land
By conspiring to surprise him.
Which we never could imagine.

He himself has twice massacred his enemy,
The Chesapeakes, whom his priests foretold
Should arise and give end to his empire.
And they foretell of a third invasion
When they should fall to strangers.

His people have good morals but, poor souls,
Are short of those *bona moralia*, which are *per se*.
They have not *in medio*, which is *in virtute.*
How can they obtain it *in ultimo,* which is *in felicitate?*
But they are healthy enough, which is *bonum corporis.*

These heathen need my redeemer, the supernal light.
Though they are not *causa regnandi*,
Yet they are *via ad regnum* and glorify His servants.
My conversion of men through fervent charity
Would be meritorious work, good work.

Mattanerew shashashewaw erowango pechecoma
Thomas Newport inoshashaw neir in hoc nantion monocock
Whe whe yah ha ha ne he wittowa wittowa

*

When Christians, being inhumanely repulsed,
Do seek to attain and maintain the right
For which they came,
May it not be lawful to possess such lands,
For Christ's sake?

It is the priests who resist our settlement,
Tell their people *Okeus* will be offended
And will not be appeased with a thousand sacrifices,
Nay a hecatomb of their children,
If they permit our teachings among them.

These priests should be taken and delivered
Like those of Baal; slain unto the last man,
In their own temple.
The Indian would be more amenable to influence
Were these seducers taken care of.

The Old Testament shows how,
When nations would not submit by fair entreaty,
They were compelled unto *ferro et flammis*.
We thus proceed to the building of a *Sanctum Sanctorum*
To His blessed name, among the infidels.

> *Mattanerew shashashewaw erowango pechecoma*
> *Pockin Simon moshasha mingon nantian tamahuck*
> *Whe whe yah ha ha ne he wittowa wittowa*

*

28

He is amazed by my bound, blank book
And that I should write upon its pages
With a feather taken from his hair.
He adorns himself with copper, paint and beads
And in vain entreats me lay my work aside.

But Cabot and Columbus are here with me tonight
To recall the marvel of the virgin traveller;
How things corporeal reward the proud heart
With sensual delights when hitherto unknown.
Do I stand in innocence, or no?

He leads me from his house to a great fire
Encircled by his heathen people
Whom the elders lead in dance.
I must record the sight:
With his savage hoard, Powhatan incants:

> *Mattanerew shashashewaw erawango pechecoma*
> *Whe Tassantassa inoshashaw yehockan pocosack*
> *Whe whe yah ha ha ne he wittowa wittowa*
>
> *Mattanerew shashashewaw erawango pechecoma*
> *Captain Newport inoshashaw neir in hoc nantion matassan*
> *Whe whe yah ha ha ne he wittowa wittowa*
>
> *Mattanerew shashashewaw erowango pechecoma*
> *Pockin Simon moshasha mingon nantian tamahuck*
> *Whe whe yah ha ha ne he wittowa wittowa*

Merrill Abroad

Old New England spills
from his silver spoon tongue,
the expansive *a* in palm, the missing *r* in star
underscoring a sweep of hands
across the heavens, boundaries questioned,
the inherited ease of sinking
into the arms of a rustic chair
and congress with men on marble steps,
all Greece and new language before him.

I paid what was owed the old kingdom
and crossed nine waves into exile.
(They were quick, those men in penny loafers,
to keep account of any depreciation.)
Here scars blend with my sun-tanned skin
that afternoon showers will cleanse.
Then I'll receive inquisitive Persian kings,
astronomers, oracles, mathematicians,
on the grounds of my new estate.

Not for the fainthearted these parlour games.
Mademoiselles and dinner party guests
flee after the first dissection and he is left
to watch blood grow cold on the scalpel.
Not quite alone – always the Trojan followers
who live to squabble outside the chamber doors –
he smears his bloodied thumb on ringlets,
across the torso, down well delineated thighs,
toes, careful to avoid Achilles' heel.

The boy diving for pearls repeatedly
has the sepia postcard allure
favoured by Edwardian archaeologists.
But on this fair head there is no price
other than what we all pay when faces
that ought to be sculpted make us dread the mirror.
He brings another oyster to the surface.
I join the ranks of tomb raiders
and photograph the booty.

Mah-jong pieces, the night's winnings,
a jigsaw muddled on its baize, the Turkish throw
far from just so, a hubblybubbly abused:
as the swollen household dreams
men in pantaloons go down to the sea
for the launch of their working day
while the perfect host, flagging by dawn,
searches casualties for a pad and pen
to record the first sail billowing.

E: As you suggested, I've demanded time alone. The
tidal pool is now my only clock, days divided by
detachment from the ocean. And I've made my study
waves until I find a sympathy, which might lie in the
moment held before they break, the comma for effect
before the storyteller's revelation: lovers found in
bed, the reading of the killer clause in old Aunt
Molly's will. And then such thunder. One is washing
in—and I'm running out of room. Much love. J

From the villa on Mount Lycabettus,
on the second Tuesday in every month at 3.00am,
he watches the ghost of Patroklos
steal between the Parthenon's columns.
It's been going on for years, this assignation,
and still they're no nearer than acquaintances.
Tonight he offers tomatoes from his vine,
the first press of olive oil, good wine,
barely enough to equal his love.

I bleed illness to my bones;
always a weakening frame.
Under the sheerest cotton
an alabaster lover sleeps.
I am Odysseus returned
to the foot of Penelope's bed,
a lesson in what's old and yearns,
reliant on the days before disfigurement
ushered doubt into play.

Let the rush of wind through trees act as chorus,
the grand funereal queen climb his pyre
and his death-song be magnificent.
Let the wind lift ashes beyond illumination—
lost in a blind heaven—
and carry them to rain on fading ships
that bear the unfaithful away;
A guilty blessing for those who believe
themselves beyond infection by lovers.

Preface

*The true bibliomaniac may contend that his pre-occupation with
condition, editions and issues, points and all the other arcane of book-
collecting frequently is of considerable importance to sober scholarship.*

If you buy a book for its content
> this is vulgar.

If you buy a book for its binding
> this is less vulgar.

If you buy a book for its printing
> this is good.

But if you buy a book for its margins,
> the pith and marrow of the page
> where gluttons hide preoccupied
> with umrahmung, blinddruck, colophons,
> signets, explicits and incipits,

if you dream to be humbled
> by folio incunabula and indulgences,

if you are made feverish by
> the *Benedictionale of St Ethelwold*
> an Aldine Petrarch on vellum
> a first Aldine *Poliphilus*
> Sweynheims
> Jensons
> even Costeriana
> illustrated Florentines such as the unique Epistole et Evangeli
> the Ulm *Ptolemy*

the Tuppo *Aesop*
the Passau *Missale*
the Sarum *Missal*
the Ingold *Das Goldene Spiel*
a Rastell edition of *The Widow Edyth*
an unrecorded *Medicines for Horses* by W. de Worde
and large-paper Gullivers,

then vulgarity is damned.

Survey

I

Murai Shizuma's The History of the Pacification of the Empire During the Reign of Meiji *with illustrations by SensaiYeitaku: 13 parts*

I.	The culling of doves on palace lawns
II.	The bringing of children before butchered fawns
III.	The ignoring then freeing of rabid hounds
IV.	The destruction of rare insect mounds
V.	The mass importation of foreign trees
VI.	The harvest of fruits by amputees
VII.	The genetic enrichment of everyday species
VIII.	The all-night burning of wheat and/or maize
IX.	The slaughter of monkeys on holy days
X.	The confiscation of sacrosanct unctions
XI.	The deployment of forests for sinister functions
XII.	The strict regulation of natural laws
XIII.	The continual recourse to probable cause

II

Almost all of the trees died, leaving a landscape of barren,
contorted skeletons. The island finally experienced winter.

Tell them the life-giving current
has been seized by a corrupting influence.

Tell them we will never again see cahows.
They have surrendered their breeding grounds.

Tell them oil-slicks combust on eroded beaches.
Foreigners panic-sell and locals stop in wonder.

Tell them, even if unfamiliar with wealth,
that insurers are barricading their doors.

And banks will not pay out. And hotels are empty.
Tell them, if you can, of your island's future.

Then tell them I am here, at the bottom of the garden.
I have been disturbed. And I am coiled.

III

Lover's Lake caused the deaths of members of the 2nd Battalion,
Queen's Royal Rifles who camped beside it to isolate themselves
from the Yellow Fever Epidemic of 1864.

> The battalion's graves
> are whitewashed every June.
>
> Then the sun shines
> brighter on the tombs,
>
> ranks grow pale,
> chiselled edges round
>
> and down at Lover's Lake
> less irony is found.

IV

His Lordship, landing, fell upon his knees and before us all made a long and silent Prayer to himself, and after, marched up into the Town where at the Gate I bowed with the Colours.

From then the spot
was Colours' Gate,
for after his Lordship
departed with his religion
we observed a renaming
of his ways made fresh as

Threadneedle Street
Greencoat Lane
Block-Print Market
Cottonbale Arch
Dyers' Bazaar and
Embroidery Circus

a surround of tapestries
drawing on hangings
by Masters, exemplars
who went the way of our Lord,
their arts and nomenclature
adapted for our own.

V

A poem embodying an imaginary message from the votary Tiru-pani Nayinār to the god Subrahmanya through the latter's peacock, to assure him of his devotion.

We've had the skink
assigned your totem,
an endangered lizard
of varnished teak hues,
refined, as its remaining
connoisseur conjectures,
by enisled separation,
requiring silence
and shelter
but mistaken
when it enters
the slow-oven cave
of a littered bottle
becoming a message
of entrapped devotion.
Should we dub you,
mockingly, Anabaptist,
as you struggle in a slime
of beer dregs and spittle?
In the appointed hour
will you respect us
as gods, we who
live in your land
and only look on?

VI

Tattoos took hold in late 19th-century Europe and America as colonialist symbols of the exotic and primitive; of the cultural "other."

for the plural you
the abstract geometries
of landscapes are tattooed
across our backs
the iconography
of habitation
winding
onto
the neck

the inheritance
of journeys ending
where the collective
heart beats for

the singular you
for whom our waists
are bound with broad linens
rich in calligraphic genealogies
and lower still concealed piercings
laced through with golden wire and beaded
with curios sanctioned to embody our intimate prayers

VII

*The moan of the sea on the breaker outside the bay, which is often
heard before rain, was likened to the roar of a hungry animal.*

we can't be denied
because this is a contract sealed
on a wind-driven spit of rock
where the eyes and mouth
of the cabin boy are shut
against the sting of salt
and the sun above
his bent head
exists only
on faith
and he believes
and believes the beast
approaching is a saviour
as much as a monster
and we moan and
fall to our knees
repentant and bleeding
before who knows what
and before what we fear

VIII

It illustrates the extent to which the icon's meaning is determined by the context in which it is placed, and its ability to subvert and destabilize the limits placed upon its meaning by such a framing.

Twelve men
with covered heads
and dressed in red
approach the icon.
Pigmented beeswax
dammer gum varnish
and the martyrs' ashes
have been sculpted
to an image of
Wālidat Allah
the god-bearer
who points
to salvation.

Twelve men
with covered heads
and dressed in red
worship an icon
smuggled into
a neutral land.
But even here
division spreads.

IX

*I am much pleased with our meeting again. There is a little property
to remind you of me when you are in a foreign land.*

A tapa cloak with a high collar, neck tie and taniko border.
A fine walking stick banded with tortoise shell,
the ferule and handle inlaid with whale ivory.
A tabua for safe passage between territories.
The first egg of the sooty to ensure
becoming a bird-man for a year.
The royal third son of our tribe,
complete with a bountiful supply
of cooking vessels and digging tools
fashioned so cleverly, as you say,
from what we have found to hand. And what we have found to hand
is bone: skull, leg, arm, jaw, say,
which we've fashioned into tools
and which your ship's crew supply
to the princes and peoples of your tribe.
Likewise our children, enticed year on year
by the wonderment of alien fashions, who ensure
in their speech and action a devaluing of our territories.
Cloaks made of mamo feathers, ear ornaments of ivory,
ceremonial necklaces of cachalot teeth and carved paua shell
are looked upon now as fripperies to be traded on our border.

X

A bronze replica of the 16th-century carving is set into the cliff where it was discovered. As the spot affords a 180-degree view of the Atlantic it is ideal as a lookout for passing ships.

on a limestone cliff
      drained even then to skeleton
            by seas and rains
            and hardened grey
      and razored
and where desiccated roots of olivewood cling
      and crab shell
            is spent by seabirds
            we theorize one sailor
      of Portuguese origin
sat looking for salvation
      in his meantime
            sharpening sticks
            to carve his mark
      that over 500 years
has diminished to debates
      over whether his T is an R
            the F a P
            and are they his or his ship's
      and is the cross a cross
and if so
      the Order of Christ proving
            Portuguese provenance
            and all the while
      in our lengthening meantime
we lose the focus
      to conjure the marvel
            of the days it took
            and how eventually he…

XI

Angell-fish, Salmon Peale, Bonetas, Stingray, Cabally, Scnappers, Hogge-fish, Sharkes, Dogge-fish, Pilcherds, Mullets, and Rock-fish, of which bee divers kinds...for which we have no names...

Where mangroves strain to sip a brackish pool
the evolution of jellyfish finds
a variant anchored
in its thousands
to bedrock
only becoming
a blooming miracle
to feed on what is filtered
through an outlet to the sound
and upon entering the pool you are blessed
with the revelry of uncountable stinging cells
anchored bodies released anonymous and electric

XII

We dare not show his Majesty what you have just written ... Do not
depress us with fears for the fate of the Armada, because in such a
cause God will make sure it succeeds.

a miniature perfume flask with a crystal dropper to disguise
rank odours from below deck

silk ties used to decorate officers' clothing, the red dye obtained
            from cochineal insects living on Mexican nopal cactus

eight-real pieces of silver, sourced in Bolivia from the famed Hill of Potsi
and minted in Lima

   agate beads, the property of South American slaves who were
            used as oarsmen to manoeuvre during battle

a Cross of a Knight of Santiago de Compostela, belonging to Don
Alonso Martinez de Leiva, gold, and red enamelled

   a salamander broach, a charm to extinguish and survive fire, made of
      South American gold and Burmese rubies, six of which are missing

an enamelled earring of Madonna and Child mounted in a later gold
setting and embellished with a large amethyst, emeralds and a single
drop pearl

      an Agnus Dei gold reliquary with 5 compartments for holding wax
      tablets that would have been stamped with an image of the Lamb of
         God, and formed from Paschal candles blessed by the Pope

an astrolabe, sounding leads, navigational dividers and clues to the existence of an astronomical compendium with lunar and solar dials, compass, and a table of cities with their latitudes

8000 stone and iron cannonballs for 5 cannons, with another 40 cannons left behind in Killybegs, County Donegal, to make room for the 800 extra men from the floundered *La Rata Santa Maria Encoronada* and *Duquesa Santa Ana*

All were on *La Girona* – a Spanish galleass with 500 crew – on October 26th, 1588, a Wednesday, a fish day, when each man would have been apportioned 6 ounces of tunning, or cod, or squid, or 5 sardines, and 3 ounces of chick peas or beans, 1 ½ ounces of oil, and a ¼ pint of vinegar. And all of this, save 5 men, sank when the ship ran aground off the northern coast of Ireland, as the remnants of God's Armada fled.

XIII

Tucker's emerald-studded gold cross was stolen and replaced
with a plastic replica. To this date this astonishing example of
shipwreck treasure has not been recovered.

> when I brushed a thigh free of sand
> the flesh had the lure of contraband
> as in a gold and emerald Spanish cross
> disturbed by a diver's hand
>
> now there's a sense of loss
> (for that muscle toned and tanned
> the warmth of which you'd understand
> if you brushed a thigh free of sand)
>
> in a cold unproven land
> where I've barely a command
> disturbed by divers hands
> pushing me to cross and re-cross
>
> a bog of asphodel and moss
> until I'm back where I began
> recovered of that warmer land
> where I brushed a thigh free of sand

A Drunk God's Departing Words

— entries in the Ulster Museum's Visitors' Book

Knowledge speaks, wisdom listens.
I want to publically proclaim
Ulster's Truly Gods Own Country.
A great place to go on the mitch.

The most exquisite museum I have visited
in this or any parallel dimension.
I'm still discovering fascinating things.
Have you seen the living sea? I coloured turtle.

I've had sex with that mummy.
Would you like to be stuffed and looked at?
Yes! An Antrepolegist's Dream.
I want to become an archaeology.

I will deff return. Even better than 10 years ago.
Brings back memories of the past when times were good.
Glorifying the imperialist/fascist slaughter of the empire.
How many Young Zulumen are there?

I think that about covers it.
I need the toilet. Where's the toilet?

The Department of Human Tissue

—for Matt Kirkham

We train our students to be technicians. If we are explaining about the abdomen we are explaining position relevant to other organs. You need to know what's behind the stomach. Where precisely *do* you put the stethoscope? We are completely pro dissection here.

Upper limb, lower limb, abdomen, pelvis, head and neck area: we can organise you to look at the exhibits and photograph what you examine. We can permit you to photograph the bones of the lower limbs exhibiting fractures but we cannot allow the bones to leave the building.

There are any number of models of the eye and brain. Stacks of plastic bones. And we have corrosion casts of kidneys, blood vessels, pancreas, liver, spleen, and, of course, the heart. All of these can be photographed and may leave the building.

There is the mummy of a four-year old girl, a gift of the Ulster Museum. You cannot photograph the mummy and she cannot leave the building. And here are the cadaveric exhibits bequeathed to the department. A select few may be photographed, but wet specimens cannot leave the building.

Look at our website regarding body donation. We went live last Friday. We have twenty bodies, give or take, per year, all from within our jurisdiction. The only criteria are that you have not died from HIV, hepatitis A or B – and some particular cancers. I will give you our e-mail for further communications.

Leviticus

—*for Iris Robinson*

I propose we make it law
and set aside this day for sinning.
Let's welcome back our bastards and castrati,
wear brazen blends of wool and linen
and allow all women who squeeze the balls
of squabbling men to keep their hands.
If you grant me this, in writing,
I will shave my hair and clip my nails,
even don the leathers. I will be your slave
and let you test me to my limits. But beware:
if I am to be your slave I cannot be for sale.
This much remains my right, despite such sinning.

Deuteronomy

This is the word I swear by.
Used in edicts and fables
it contains the influence of stars,
the raising of great stones,
the telling of tales by firelight to innocents.
And I employ it in our mythology of love—
but have kept this secret
as you would never accept the idolatry.
Its powers have been witnessed
when included in our sacred ballads:
our golden effigies are borne
above the crowd by crazed acolytes
privy to our covenant, and, most agreeably,
denounced by prophets feeding off the old ways.

Of the Vein

There beyond the green check lawn, the group
who keep to shade and doff their boaters
to the beauties but fix an eye or eight
on passers by to warn them of a boundary.

Says John to James: *Dates, figs and plums, old chum:*
Look you there on deserts spread on a picnic blanket.

Here one adds, as one must,
some rolling thunder.

James to John: *I hear, when it rains, Japanese ladies*
invert their parasols to catch chrysanthemums.

One elder wanders off,
as eventually one must.
From underneath a willow tree
he leads his boy to bed and to obituaries.

Matt to Tom: *When bird watching, I use opera glasses*
to spy the best throated, don't you know.

And so the code continues:
here two dashes, there a dot,
passed down the generations
or in lapel carnations pinned by practised hands.

Matt to James to John to Tom (perhaps in Greek with masks):
Four marble peacocks move and shape their own mythologies.

Here one adds, as one must,
some desperate laughter.

Tom to John to Matt to James (perhaps en masse they gesture):
Let's raise a finger to detractors.

Now, there beyond the green check lawn,
only parts survive. There there now.
A high brow, an elegant calf, a digit raised,
displayed like this. (And here I gesture.)

Or, as if there'd been a choice, a neck
set at an angle ripe for striking, muscles flexed
by an adoring sculptor, veins plumped
and fit for bursting. Green. Reclaimed.

I say: *I inherit the vainglorious.*

On Mastroianni in *A Special Day*

The world, Marcello, has gone outside
to witness Adolph hold hands with Benito.
We have watched your booted and tasselled neighbours
running to become the newsreel's throng.
But I linger with you, at a simple table,
our backs to the state apartment's view.
And I will mirror you:
let us rest our chins once more
on the back of our hands and sigh.
Like this, I will fall for you again,
the face that pretends a *curriculum vitae*
of macho bravado, betrayed by its history –
the cheeks too quick to blush, the lips to tremble.

Together we define the *ipsissima verba* for entrapment,
which leads to the problem of filling our time.
So you grind beans for a last cup of coffee,
lend me your *Three Musketeers* for escape
and we dance the rumba once more as an act of defiance.

Hold me tight and pilot me up to the tower block's roof
where we can display ourselves above all of Rome.
Two men among immaculate avenues of boiled-white sheets,
we will move from back projected silhouettes
to abandon ourselves in the levelling glare of sunlight
where our secret must slip. Listen for the fall.
But just this once, Marcello, I will be allowed
to wrap you in cotton and steal you from harm,
to smuggle you into an alien city
where we will be free to dance the latest craze
with legions of courageous d'Artagnans.

Shorts

Untitled

Between bottles, I'd kill time in galleries
looking for the perfect form in which to drown.
A few Ophelias and I'd be tickled pink,
tipsy with pity and ready for the drink.

A Little Britten

Grimes has thrown his name to the waves
and finds his mind retreats to childhoods
lost in accidental circumstances to the sea.

Puberty

The daughter to the music teacher
sotto voce hums a tune
her mother did not give her.

A Dedication

Spread bleached vellum sheets on snow
and consecrate the spot that made our love distinguished.

Three for Robin Wood (1931–2009)

The Hitch

Freudian Marxists are always hungry.
A dilemma: Grace Kelly enters,
complete with a bourgeois dinner.

Divertissement

Divorced from context
(no Oedipal son,
no wailing mother),
Cavillieri Rusticana's
Intermezzo plays:

a broken danseur
downstage-
left in motley,
arms limp first
position, spotlit
like the Dying
Swan: De Niro's
Jake La Motta.

The Searcher

Enter, Ethan, and steal familial comforts
from domesticated trails,

survey nieces' frames and chart the alteration
of terrain in nephews' faces,

trek from kitchen to communal table
then desecrate your brother's bed.

Eradicate his claim. Bolt the door.
Leave the sun outside to bake your dead.

Lullaby for Rock

Darling, there's a deer at the window.
But there you lie, divine and unconscious.
Will you ever recall that you fell from the rock face
in your headlong rush to stop my leaving?

It's really too comic: you, the ardent young lover;
me, the guilt-ridden widow; a snow covered scene;
and tremulando violins scoring your arc through the air.
(Reviewing it frame by frame it appears you bounce!)

When you wake to my face an inch from yours,
lipstick and pancake retouching complete,
will I confess straightaway why I'm back at the mill?
Or will you guess, Darling? Do I glow? You see:

> *The children have given their blessing,*
> *the tested best friend is true,*
> *the man-of-my-years is sent packing*
> *and I'm devoting myself just to you.*

All His World Allows

—after Douglas Sirk and Todd Haynes

INTERIOR: NIGHT. *In some noir-lit downtown bar a man reads Proust for a cliché while in a tight red T-shirt a muscular teen lounges in a leatherette booth and reads the room. A stranger's describing a gown:*

> Crimson taffeta with black lace trim,
> backdropped by autumnal gardens. My wife,
> Cathy, bleeding into memory and fixing.

It's a generation since the clientele changed and his continual downing of Scotch has led pokerfaced men to be wary:

> She wore it the night of our fall from splendour,
> our imitation lives laid bare. Old pals
> interrupted the practiced flow of company
> parties to stare. Refilling martinis had to be
> postponed.

He smiles the half-smile of the blamed:

> But I emerged from her shadow *In Glorious
> Melodrama!* Rock had been exposed.

Out of the home and joining the game, he couldn't have gone for one of the queens, the group of brave young radicals. Not yet. My look and my suit are his safety zone. Conformity's still an attraction.

The Last Picture Show on DVD

Picture Show is 30 years old, and it doesn't seem like such a long time, on some level. Time, according to that old cliché, is deeply relative.

— Peter Bogdonovich

105:40: A poker-straight road bisecting flatlands. Beat-up sedans are heading for the graduates' picnic. Whooping it up, future plaid flannel and 501 oilhands are assembling the high school clans.

When they arrive the view will be green—until the pairing of jocks and squares with girls they'd only casually considered as wives implants both sides with a dread of fixed agendas.

Mid-shot: Sonny stares out of the Ford's backseat window, divorced from his best friend's show of bravado at being the choice no one doubts is destined for the small-town beauty queen.

Sonny's POV: the fishing hole's chromium sheen, the location of the proverbial scene where the wise Ol'-Lion-Sam, baiting his hook, once had the apprenticing Sonny's rapt attention.

Here Sam spun the story of an old young love: him and his sweetheart and how they'd rented some time in the fantasyland of an epic summer; of skinny-dipping, dreams and an unresolved ending:

"One day she wanted to swim the horses ... She bet me a silver dollar she could beat me ... I bet she still got that silver dollar ... Being crazy 'bout a woman like her is always the right thing to do."

*

Juan Ugarte was my Sam: Traveller, Dancer and Alice's Lover. We met in Denver and I fell for him fast. When he asked, I sank my last dollar into an old Ford truck and we fled. Just us. It was San Francisco or bust.

On our way he analysed my *tours en l'air* and turns in general. I couldn't find the balance needed of a beautifully arched foot for the tricks I'd seen him perform in his *pas de deux*.

"But I'm convinced your body is for dancing … The way you hold the hands in *à la seconde*, how you master breath … And you only see the image in the mirror."

We turned off a Rocky Mountain pass and he asked me to dance barefoot in linen snow. He inspected each fresh-fossilled step to remedy my imperfections.

As an expression of hope, this was my long-shot proverbial. So, we cried for different causes when we changed gears, leaving the mountains for the dawn of a John Ford set.

He'd just said that he caught the same desert reds in the fiery hair of his Alice back home. Or bust. When we finally met up, me and the intuitive woman prickled.

*

They buried Ol' Sam on top of a hill. Our last-dollar truck rusted on blocks. Beat-up sedans are heading for the graduates' picnic. In the backseat, Sonny is drying his eyes. 106:08. Just under thirty seconds.

Full Moon in Brooklyn

I first saw the boy who's in my head
on a summer's night when he danced
for relative strangers on a Brooklyn dock.
A granddame's nieces in vanilla silk dresses
finished pirouetting, applause politely
beyond polite. Caught in the social brinkmanship
of Sheepshead Bay, ice rattled in highballs
summoned him to perform. All right, he was
overweight, the music disposable pop,
the dock was not sprung, but he leapt.
The boy who's in my head leapt and spun.
And in the silence without applause
he bowed not to us but turned to welcome
thousands of horseshoe crabs, inching ashore.

On the Pier

The contrail divides a late September sky
joining dots along a line from here
north-north-east to Scotland. Does High Kells,
Carrine, Campbeltown or Carradale
act as pivot when the line drifts west?
Whichever. It dissipates in half an hour—
perhaps a little more. But in that time
I've filled a memory stick with photographs,
one gigabyte of a harbour's evening business:
crab-potters' keels scraped while owners chat
around the tides and times, a muddied spaniel
barking at turnstones, and the 'Celestine',
an old boat bright against the water's grey,
varnished trim, polished brass and anchored.

Harbour

Groomsport's tenders settle to their weightier sides.
Plastic oil-carton buoys float inches above slack rope cables.
The derelict trawler, 'Red Shamrock', finally gets the joke
and beneath its prow a man in oilskins digs for bait
remembering when harbours drew sons to their fathers.
As the last emphasis of evening pinks the Copeland Islands
and the lighthouse stutters,
retired couples in cars fold the final edition
and head home for convenience store teas.

A seal comes up for air in the bay.
Three kids skipping stones arrest their arms mid throw
and follow its progress with cartoon stealth tactics,
betting on where it's likely to surface.
They descend the ladder at the end of the pier
and in the spill of a Gatsby-green landing light,
like sailors in rigging, hold on with one hand and lean out,
loyal until the seal is at large in the Irish Sea.
The lighthouse flares. The Copelands opal.

Scoil

A gifted accordion player whose left hand
can't match what's produced by the right
flattens the left across bass buttons to produce
a chord deliberately beyond dissonance—
the equivalent, someone suggests over dinner,
of outer Hebridean congregations who
when fed measures by upstanding soloists
contribute glosses unharmonious to our ears' ken.

Talk drifts to musicians' quirks: the flautist
who speaks with his hands dancing beside his head;
'Head-and-Shoulders' who articulates every syllable
with a twitch; the singer who uses his index finger
to sketch the accents and rhythms of songs.
And we debate why musicians lean in to clasp
another's hand. Is it a custom dragged
from the dark around the hearth?

Two-to-my-right proposes a drum supplies
the same contribution as the flattened left.
And is this not, I ask, like the piper's drone?
No! chorus the eight around the table.
The drone is a chartable tone. Think Stockhausen
and cherished cacophony. And did I know
players omit notes for effect on the inward
and outward motion of the bellows? I did not.

The Old New Regime

Say, whatever this is, it's like
Aunt Bridget's make-up routine,
the one she applies for Fridays
in the old resented town.

Or perhaps we could say it's like
walking the neighbour's Chihuahua,
the proverbial burden bequeathed
by a distant relation on his mother's side.

Or, for the sake of having an argument,
let's say it's a List of Essential CDs,
some Godforsaken Dock, or that new familiar,
the Flickering Neon Sign.

Anything. As long as you think
it's indifferent and hip it won't matter.
colloquial brilliance will blind
and we'll miss that $X = Y$

by only the slightest of designs.
Which brings us back to Aunt Bridget
and her pink glitter eye shadow.
A shade, shall we say, in decline?

Lines at Lacken Mill

How lovely it is today!
The sunlight breaks and flickers
On the margin of my book.
  —9th-Century Irish marginalia

The shower has passed but rain
drops from the canopy to play the river like a drum
and I'm absorbed by the performance
of a wayward beat falling on the page.
The *a* in apple blossoms and the *b*
in beauty blooms, infecting with the bleed
all well-meaning words.
                    And just as well.

For I would tell you simply
that the mill cat rests beside me, the dog
transfixed by swans. I would write
of an ancient weir broking for a race;
of herds pastured for millennia
lapping waters that a heron scours;
of the Erne's remorseless measure
over worn, familial rocks
and of eddies they maintain for dedicated salmon.
I would even reach and reference linnet's wings
but you have heard all this and are immune.

Perhaps a fashion's passed
as these spots in time diminish.
Still, I'll take some pleasure
from the seamless finish:
a single note magnificat,
climax to the great tympanic act,
falls then fades in the quickening river.

And now the page is parched. Old *a*'s and *b*'s
that advocated venture have been stemmed.
But you, attuned to perfect labours, prove
dried blooms and blossoms will be shamed
when, shortly, we will witness birth again.

Counterpoint

—*after Conor O'Callaghan*

Place something on the windowsill
before we get to swallows in the evening sky,
something between you and the sovereignty of air:
week-old roses, silver-framed relations,
or an old milk jug, chipped Cornish ware.
You choose, but it should be noted
as you're opening the mail, look up,
and make a little from the fact it's framed
by more than fabric: hand-washed nets become
the history of lace as it pertains to family,
or in that vein, the fading luxuries of velvets.
And as the swallows flit, of course like memories,
here you'll neatly segue to your close.
recall old dialogues, spot the stranger passing.

Ken,

The enclosed CD is for playing
on the drive north from Toronto
into the puzzle of lakes, for when
you near the old Spruce Winds farm
and picture Jon in his flannel shirt
splitting logs. For this I'd suggest
the melancholic shelter of a slow air:
The Girl that Broke My Heart.
And if you turn down the lane, roll
to a stop, catching the breath-of-him
as he skates to a blur on the frozen pond,
plump for a track with real zip:
John Naughton's Green Mountain /
Welcome Here Again. The two of them reels.

Effacé

– for Nora

Yours was the face I almost lived a lie for,
that might have brought about the 2.4,
not this sterile A4 annual report
about the daughter's aptitude for sport,
Ted's reunion and the dress you wore.

I want to know: did the dress allow
seductive *développés* and *port de bras*,
did sling-backs reveal triumphant arches,
were accountants left unconscious
and the husband damning Terpsichore?

But should I be content if my Odette
is happy to distract suburban courts?
Nibble canapés my swan, forget
this mincing prince who hoped we might be more.

Retreat

I've built us a house from hand-cut limestone
and stacked the blocks without mortar.
Accrued weight is the only chance they'll get.

Our floorboards are of rare untreated cedar,
pegged and laid over bleached coral sand.
I'll leave you to ponder the benefits of staining.

I've forgone electricity, opting to hoard
two hundred boxes of slow-burning candles, ten to a box.
Wood for the oven is drying out against the beach wall.

The oven is functional, the cooler exotically stocked.
In the dining room is a painted table with only two chairs.
Follow the logic: there's one queen-size in the one bedroom.

And propriety needs me to report there's no glass
in the window frames: what you thought
you saw through so clearly was, is, air. Say 'Ah....'

I'll bring my wardrobe, if you care to dress for dinner,
but there are no mirrors anywhere, of any kind,
no reflective surfaces of any sort. Like this, I will be fine.

I've had the roof lime-washed to the point
where rainwater is sufficiently filtered
to provide the softest supply for bubble baths.

That lofty ambition complete, I've tried out some names:
Cove Edge, *Beachcomber's Hut*, *Blue Horizons*.
But at this time of life, and given our circumstance,

let's live with the sign on the gate: KEEP OUT! *Renaissance*.

Notes

Marginalia (4)

After an anonymous 9th-Century Irish monastic work, sometimes given the title 'The Blackbird of Belfast Lough'.

Recension (14-18)

Section 1: the italicised couplets are traditional Bermudian verse.

Ferro et Flammis (26-29)

Based on the writings of William Strachey (1572-1621). See *The Historie of Travaile into Virginia Britannia,* c. 1618, ed. R.H. Major (London: Hakluyt Society, 1849), in which Strachey records the early Jamestown settlers' experiences and transcribes the language of the tribes of the great chief Powhatan. The quoted song is believed to be an expression of anger against the Tassantassa (the English settlers) and a commemoration of the killing of Thomas Newport and capture of Simon Score. See Robert Stevenson's article, "English Sources for Indian Music Until 1882" in *Ethnomusicology* 17.3 (1973): 399-442. It is also worth noting that Strachey's firsthand report of the wreck of the *Sea Venture* on Bermuda's reef (1609) became something of a sensation when it reached London. Indeed, it is said to have inspired Shakespeare to write *The Tempest*. All those aboard the *Sea Venture* survived. Claiming the uninhabited island for the Crown, they built two ships and somewhat reluctantly continued on to Jamestown. John Rolfe, whose wife and infant child died while in Bermuda, went on to marry Pocahontas, daughter of Powhatan.

Preface (33-34)

Based on writings found in: William Bond, ed., *Records of a Bibliographer: Selected Papers of William Alexander Jackson* (Cambridge: Belknap Press of Harvard University Press, 1967).

Survey (35-48)

Sources of epigraphs (edited, occasionally):

- Section I: Robert Kennedy Douglas, ed., *Catalogue of Japanese Printed Books and Manuscripts of the Library of the British Museum* (London: British Museum, 1989).
- Sections II, III, IV, VI, VII, X, XIII: Ian McDonald-Smith, *A Scape to Bermuda* (Bermuda: Just Clicked Publications, 1991).
- Section V: L.D. Barnett, ed., *A Supplementary Catalogue of the Tamil Books in the Library of the British Museum* (London: British Museum, 1931).
- Section VIII: Fiona Richards, "The Desecrated Shrine: Moveable Icons and Literary Irreverence in Salman Rushdie's 'The Prophet's Hair'," *SOAS Literary Review 2* (Summer 2000), 18 May 2010 <http://www.soas.ac.uk/soaslit/2000_index.htm>.
- Section IX: Winifred Glover, *Polynesia* (Belfast: Ulster Museum, 1986).
- Section XI: William Strachey, "A True Reportory of the Wreck and Redemption of Sir Thomas Gates, Knight," 15. Jul. 1610 (London: Samuel Purchas, 1625).
- Section XIII: The Ulster Museum, Belfast, "The Armada Collection."

The Last Picture Show on DVD (61-62)

"One day she wanted to swim the horses" through to "right thing to do" is from the film. Script by James Lee Barrett, Peter Bogdonovich, Larry McMurtry and Polly Platt (not credited). Directed by Peter Bogdonovich (1971).